RISING FROM THE ASHES

INSPIRATIONAL STORIES OF TRIUMPH OVER ADVERSITY

INKWELL NOMAD

"This book is dedicated to the readers who seek inspiration and motivation to overcome challenges and reach their goals. We hope that the stories within these pages will serve as a reminder that anything is possible, and that with determination and hard work, you too can achieve your dreams. May these stories be a source of encouragement and hope as you navigate your own journey, and may they inspire you to reach new heights and live your best life."

Contents

Preface

We all look for stories that motivate us and remind of the wonderous possibilities of human endeavours. They bring newfound perspective, energy and examples for individual applications in life.

In this collection of 24 motivational real-life stories, I have compiled a diverse set of narratives that showcase the triumph of the human spirit over adversity. Each story is a testament to the power of determination, hard work, and the resilience of the human mind and body.

As you read through these pages, you will be inspired by the incredible journeys of individuals who have faced seemingly insurmountable obstacles and come out on top. From overcoming physical disabilities, to achieving success in business, and even climbing the highest peaks in the world, these stories will remind you that anything is possible with the right mindset and attitude. The individuals are chosen from diverse backgrounds and cultures to bring you a holistic global collection of stories. They are categorized under different obstacles to success that one can call so in life.

These stories also serve as a reminder that we all have the potential to achieve great things, regardless of our background or circumstances. They demonstrate that with the right mindset and approach, we can all overcome the obstacles that stand in our way and achieve our goals.

So, let these stories be a source of inspiration as you embark on your own journey, and may they remind you to never give up on your dreams.

Acknowledgements

With love and gratitude to my Spouse & Daughter...!

And of course, forever respect and gratitude to the heroes of this book whose magnificent and inspirational life stories you are about to read...!

CHAPTER ONE

DISABILITY

Disability can present a number of challenges that may make it more difficult for an individual to achieve success in certain areas of life. Some of these challenges may include:

1. Physical barriers: People with disabilities may face physical barriers that prevent them from accessing certain places, activities, or opportunities. This can limit their ability to work, learn, and participate in their communities.
2. Attitudinal barriers: People with disabilities may also face discrimination and negative attitudes from others, which can create additional obstacles to achieving success.
3. Limited access to resources: People with disabilities may have limited access to resources such as education, healthcare, and technology that can help them achieve success.
4. Socio-economic disparities: People with disabilities are more likely to live in poverty and face socio-economic disparities, which can make it difficult for them to achieve success.

5. Difficulty in finding employments: People with disabilities may face difficulties in finding employment due to lack of accessibility, discrimination and lack of understanding of their abilities.

6. Difficulty in accessing education: People with disabilities may face difficulties in accessing education due to lack of accessibility, lack of appropriate accommodations and lack of understanding of their needs.

7. Difficulty in maintaining social connections: People with disabilities may face difficulties in maintaining social connections due to lack of accessibility, discrimination and lack of understanding of their abilities.

While these challenges can make it more difficult for people with disabilities to achieve success, many individuals with disabilities have been able to overcome these obstacles and achieve great success in their lives. This chapter brings you the stories of individuals who made examples for generations to come.

STEVIE WONDER

"You will never feel proud of your work if you find no joy within it; your best work is always joyful work."

— Stevie Wonder

Stevie Wonder in 1994

Few pop culture icons have been as enduringly popular and impactful as Stevie Wonder. From his beginnings as a child prodigy in the 1960s to his long-running career that stretches into the present day, Wonder has impressed generations of music listeners with his stunning musical versatility and astounding vocal range.

Stevie Wonder, born Stevland Hardaway Morris, was born in Saginaw, Michigan, on May 13, 1950. He was born six weeks premature and as a result, he was born with a condition called retinopathy of prematurity, which caused him to become blind. At the age of four, Wonder's parents divorced, and he struggled due to poverty with five siblings and only the mother - making his childhood more difficult.

Despite these challenges, Stevie Wonder managed to find joy in his music.

At the age of seven, Stevie Wonder began attending the Michigan School for the Blind where he developed his talents further as a musician. He learned to play several instruments, including the piano, drums, harmonica, and saxophone. He also began singing and composing his own music.

At the age of 11, Stevie Wonder was discovered by Ronnie White of the Motown group The Miracles, and he was signed to Motown Records. He released his first album, "The Jazz Soul of Little Stevie" under the name Little Stevie Wonder, and quickly gained fame and success as a child prodigy.

Despite the challenges he faced growing up, Stevie Wonder never let his blindness hold him back. He continued to pursue his love of music, and through hard work and dedication, he became one of the most successful and influential musicians in history.

When it comes to creating music, Stevie Wonder is a true renaissance man. He is a virtuoso on multiple instruments, including the piano, drums, and harmonica, and he is also a skilled singer, songwriter, and producer. In addition to his musical talents, Wonder is also known for his positive attitude and commitment to excellence.

Wonder's process of creating music is one that is rooted in passion and positivity. He has said that he always begins with the intention of making something that will make people happy. From there, he allows the music to flow through him, trusting in his instincts and intuition to guide the way. The result is always something truly special that resonates with listeners on a deep level.

Whether he's crafting a new song or performing one of his classics, Stevie Wonder always brings his signature joy and positive vibes to the table. It's this commitment to excellence and positivity that makes him one of the most beloved musicians of all time.

Stevie Wonder is widely considered to be one of the greatest musicians of all time, with a career that spans over six decades. Some of the pinnacle moments in his career include:

- 1972 Album "Music of My Mind": This was Stevie's first album to fully showcase his talents as a multi-instrumentalist and songwriter. It was a critical success and helped establish him as one of the most innovative and important musicians of his generation.
- 1976 Album "Songs in the Key of Life": Considered by many as his greatest work, this double album was a commercial and critical success. It earned Stevie four Grammy Awards, including Album of the Year, and has been included in many "greatest albums of all time" lists.
- 1985 "We Are the World": Stevie co-wrote and sang on this charity single, which was released to raise money for famine relief in Africa. The song was a massive commercial success and helped raise millions of dollars for the cause.
- 1991 "Superstition" - Stevie Wonder's hit single "Superstition" is considered one of the greatest songs of all time. The single was released in 1972 and topped charts worldwide and was also a commercial success.

With a net worth of $200 million, Wonder continues to perform, write, and record music today. He has been honored with numerous awards and accolades, along with 25 Grammy Awards, an Academy Award for Best Original Song Score (for The Woman in Red), and a Presidential Medal of Freedom and been inducted into the Rock & Roll Hall of Fame, received the prestigious Kennedy Center Honors for his lifetime achievement in music.

NICK VUJICIC

"Don't put your life on hold so that you can dwell on the unfairness of past hurts."

— Nick Vujicic

Nick Vujicic is a renowned motivational speaker, author, and evangelist. Born without limbs and with a genetic disorder known as tetra-amelia syndrome, he has been an inspiration to many people around the world. Despite his physical limitations, Nick has achieved amazing feats and made a positive impact on the lives of many.

Nick Vujicic was born on the 4th of December in the year 1982, in Australian metro Melbourne. His parents were both immigrants who had come to Australia from Yugoslavia in the 1970s. Nick was born with a rare condition called tetra-amelia syndrome, which caused him to be born without any limbs.

Nick Vujicic in 2021

As a child, Nick faced many challenges and obstacles. His early childhood was not that kind with his peers bullying and teasing Nick. He felt isolated and alone for long. However, he refused to let his condition get the best of him. With the support of his family and friends, Nick learned to embrace who he was and not allow his disability to define him.

He went on to attend school and get an education. In 2005, he graduated from Griffith University with a degree in commerce and a double major in accounting and financial planning. Nick is now a successful motivational speaker, author, and entrepreneur. He travels all over the world sharing his story and inspiring others to overcome their own challenges.

The process of excellence is a lifelong journey that requires dedication and commitment. It is not something that can be achieved overnight, but rather is something that must be worked towards day after day, week after week, month after month, and year after year.

The first step on the road to excellence is to set high standards for oneself. This means having specific goals and objectives that one is striving to achieve. It is important to remember that these goals should be realistic and achievable; otherwise they will only serve to discourage and demotivate.

Once personal standards have been set, it is then necessary to start taking action towards achieving them. This may involve making changes in one's lifestyle, such as eating healthier or exercising more regularly. It may also require studying harder or practicing more frequently. Whatever the case may be, it is important to put in the effort required to reach the level of excellence desired.

The final step in the process of excellence is to never give up. There will inevitably be setbacks and obstacles along the way, but it is important to persevere through these challenges. Giving up will only lead to regret; staying the course and continuing to strive for success will lead to a sense of accomplishment and pride. Nick did exactly this to become a successful example for the entire world for generations.

Despite the challenges he's faced in life, Nick has become a successful author, motivational speaker, and business owner. He is an inspiration to people all over the world who are facing difficulties in their lives.

In his youth, Nick struggled with depression and suicidal thoughts but eventually found hope and purpose in his faith. He started speaking about his experiences and sharing his positive outlook on life, which has helped millions of people worldwide.

Nick has written several books about his life and how he overcame the odds to achieve success. Some of them are,

1. "Life Without Limits: Inspiration for a Ridiculously Good Life" - This is Nick's memoir, in which he shares his personal story of overcoming adversity and challenges to achieve success and happiness. He also offers advice and inspiration for readers who are facing their own struggles.

2. "Unstoppable: The Incredible Power of Faith in Action" - This book is a guide for readers to develop an unshakable faith in themselves and in God. It is a combination of Nick's personal stories, biblical teachings and practical advice.

3. "Stand Strong: You Can Overcome Bullying (and Other Stuff That Keeps You Down)" - In this book Nick addresses the issue of bullying and how to overcome it. Nick shares his own experiences from being bullied in his childhood and advise on how one can develop self-confidence in adversity.

4. "Be the Hands and Feet: Living out God's Love for All His Children" - This book is a call to action, encouraging readers to be the hands and feet of Jesus, by serving others and making a difference in the world. Nick shares his own experiences of service and offers practical advice for readers who want to get involved in serving others.

He is also the founder of Life Without Limbs, an organization that provides support and resources for people with disabilities. He is now an inspiration to people all over the world who are facing difficulties in their lives.

CHRISTY BROWN

"You touched my flawed life so gently with loveburning upward in dark steady flameburning me, burning me into healing."

— Christy Brown, Of Snails and Skylarks

Christy Brown is an inspirational figure who overcame great odds to achieve success. Born with a disability, Chris had difficulty engaging in everyday activities. Despite his disability, Christy developed a passion for writing, art and literature that drove him forward and allowed him to make his mark on society.

Christy Brown in 1954

In this article, we will explore the life of Christy Brown and how he managed to turn his disability into an opportunity for success. We will look at the inspiring story of a young man from Dublin who used his determination to create a unique legacy that continues to bring joy and inspiration today.

Christy Brown was born in Dublin, Ireland, on June 5th, 1932. His parents were working class and he was one of thirteen children. Christy had cerebral palsy and as a result, he was unable to walk or talk. Christy's father, Paddy

Brown, was determined that his son would not be limited by his disability and encouraged him to use whatever abilities he did have. Christy began to paint and write with his left foot and soon started to gain recognition for his talent. He was educated at home by his mother until he was nine years old, when he started attending a special school for children with disabilities. He then went on to study at Dublin's Central Technical Institute and Trinity College.

Christy Brown went on to become a multi-talented individual, despite having cerebral palsy which limited his movement and communication. He produced a variety of works throughout his life, including:

1. Writing: Brown wrote an autobiography, "My Left Foot", which was published in 1954. The book was a critical success and was later adapted into a film of the same name, which won several awards, including the Academy Award for Best Actor for Daniel Day-Lewis.
2. Painting: Brown used his left foot to paint pictures, and his artwork was exhibited in galleries in Ireland and London. His paintings were a mix of abstract and figurative styles and were widely recognized for their expressiveness and uniqueness.
3. Poetry: Brown wrote poetry throughout his life and some of his work has been published in various anthologies. His poetry is characterized by its depth and emotional intensity, reflecting on his own experiences and the struggles he faced as a person with a disability.
4. Advocating: Brown was a passionate advocate for people with disabilities, and worked to promote their rights and inclusion in society. He was a strong voice for the disabled community and was an inspiration to many.

5. Acting: Brown appeared in the film adaptation of his autobiography "My Left Foot" in 1989. He was also an actor in the community theater, performing in several plays.

His work has served as a powerful message of hope and inspiration to people with disabilities and others who face challenges in their lives. His paintings and poetry are still exhibited and remembered.

Throughout his life, Brown continued to write, paint and create poetry. He was also a passionate advocate for people with disabilities and worked to promote their rights and inclusion in society. He passed away in 1981, at the age of 49, but his legacy continues to inspire people around the world.

In order to achieve success in anything you do, Christy Brown recommends the following: first and foremost, develop a solid work ethic; be relentless in your pursuit of excellence; set yourself apart from the competition; surround yourself with positive people who will help you reach your goals; and always continue to learn and grow. These are just a few of the many pieces of advice that Christy Brown has for those looking to achieve success in their lives. By following these simple tips, you too can find success in whatever you set your mind to.

CHAPTER TWO

AGE

Age can be perceived as an obstacle to success by some people because society often associates youth with energy, creativity, and innovation. However, age is not a determinant factor for success, as many older individuals have achieved great things later in life. In order to overcome any potential obstacles that age may present, it is important to focus on one's strengths and abilities, rather than dwelling on any perceived limitations.

Additionally, individuals can overcome age as an obstacle by keeping an open mind, continue learning and adapting to new technologies and skills, maintain a positive attitude, and surround themselves with people who inspire and support them. It's also important to stay physically and mentally healthy, and have a sense of purpose.

It's important to remember that age is just a number, and success is not determined by how old someone is, but rather by their drive, determination, and willingness to work hard and persevere in the face of challenges.

JULIA CHILD

"Find something you're passionate about and keep tremendously interested in it."

— Julia Child

Julia Child in 1978

Julia Child was an American chef, author, and television personality who is best known for introducing French cuisine to American audiences. She was born in Pasadena, California in 1912 and grew up in a wealthy family. After graduating from Smith College, she worked in advertising and then joined the Office of Strategic Services (OSS) during World War II.

It was during her time in Europe with her husband, Paul Child, that she developed a love for French cuisine. She attended Le Cordon Bleu cooking school in Paris and then studied with renowned chefs such as Simone Beck and Louisette Bertholle.

Julia Child began her culinary career at the age of 50. She had moved to France with her husband Paul Child and while living there she developed an interest in French cuisine. She attended Le Cordon Bleu cooking school in Paris and then studied with renowned chefs such as Simone Beck and Louisette Bertholle. After learning the techniques and skills of French cooking, she returned to the United States and co-wrote "Mastering the Art of French Cooking" with Simone Beck and Louisette Bertholle, the book was published in 1961 which became a bestseller and is still considered a classic in the culinary world. The book was written for American housewives and aimed to demystify French cooking and make it accessible to a wider audience.

In 1963, she began hosting her own cooking show, "The French Chef," which ran for more than a decade and made her a household name. She went on to host several other cooking shows and wrote several more cookbooks. Julia Child was also a vocal advocate for culinary education and helped establish several culinary schools in the United States. She passed away in 2004, but her legacy lives on through her cookbooks, television shows, and the countless individuals she inspired to love and appreciate good food.

Julia Child was known for her practical and down-to-earth approach to cooking. She believed that anyone could learn to cook and that the key to success in the kitchen was to have confidence and not be afraid to make mistakes. She often emphasized the importance of using high-quality ingredients and taking the time to properly prepare them. Some of her most famous advice includes:

- "Learn how to cook - try new recipes, learn from your mistakes, be fearless, and above all have fun!"
- "Always start with a good recipe and good ingredients."
- "The only real stumbling block is fear of failure. In cooking, you've got to have a what-the-hell attitude."
- "You don't have to cook fancy or complicated masterpieces - just good food from fresh ingredients."
- "Find something you're passionate about and keep tremendously interested in it."
- "The best way to execute French cooking is to get good and loaded and whack the hell out of a chicken. Bon appétit."
- "Always remember: If you're alone in the kitchen and you drop the lamb, you can always just pick it up. Who's going to know?"
- "The measure of achievement is not winning awards. It's doing something that you appreciate, something you believe is worthwhile."

Age was never an obstacle in her life - with networth of ~$50 million she just loved what she was doing and propagated the same to the world setting an example for generations that were to come.

GEORGE DAWSON

"Things will be alright. People need to hear that. Life is good, just as it is. There isn't anything that I would change about my life."

— George Dawson, Life is So Good

George Dawson in 2000

George Dawson was an American author, motivational speaker and civil rights activist, born in Texas in 1898. He was born into slavery and spent most of his life working in different jobs, such as a farmer, construction worker, and a rail worker. Despite his difficult life, he always had an interest in learning how to read and write, but didn't have the opportunity to do so until he was 98 years old.

George Dawson's learned how to read and write at the age of 98. He had always had an interest in learning how to read and write, but never had the opportunity to do so until he was 98 years old. He was taught by a young teacher named Richard Glaubman, who was writing a book about Dawson's life. George Dawson was so excited to learn how to read that, despite his age, he would stay up late at night reading and writing. This incident changed his life and opened many doors for him, and he went on to become an author, motivational speaker and civil rights activist.

George Dawson became an inspiration to many people, especially to older adults and children, when his memoir was published in 2000. He became a sought-after speaker and was even invited to the White House, where he met President Bill Clinton. George Dawson passed away in 2001, but his legacy lives on through his book, which continues to inspire and motivate people of all ages.

George Dawson was not a professional speaker or writer and his advice was mostly based on his personal experience and wisdom. However, some of the advice that he shared in his book "Life is So Good" and in the speeches he gave are:

- "Learn to read, it will open doors and change your life."
- "Don't let age be a barrier, you're never too old to learn something new."
- "Be persistent, if you want something bad enough, you'll find a way to get it."
- "Be grateful for what you have, it's easy to take things for granted."

- "Don't let setbacks stop you, keep going and you'll reach your goals."
- "Be kind to others, it's one of the most important things you can do."
- "Life is good, enjoy it and make the most of it."
- "Don't be afraid to ask for help, there are people who care and want to help."
- "Be patient, good things come to those who wait."
- "Believe in yourself, you have the power to change your life."

He left behind a powerful message that age is not a barrier to success and that it's never too late to learn something new. He showed us that with determination, perseverance, and a positive attitude, anything is possible.

COLONEL SANDERS

"The hard way builds solidly a foundation of confidence that cannot be swept away."

— Colonel Sanders

Colonel Harland Sanders was a man who many know for his iconic white suit and the delicious fried chicken he created. However, there is much more to the story of this American icon.

Colonel Sanders in 1974

Sanders was born on September 9, 1890 in Henryville, Indiana and was raised on a farm. He was the oldest of three children and worked hard from a young age, taking on a variety of jobs throughout his youth, including as a farmhand, a streetcar conductor, and a steamboat pilot.

In his early 30s, Sanders began working as a salesman for a company that sold tires and later as a service station operator. It was during this time that Sanders began to experiment with cooking. He would often cook food for travelers who stopped at his service station in Corbin, Kentucky. Sanders would serve meals such as country ham, steak, and fried chicken.

In the 1930s, Sanders opened his first restaurant, the Sanders Court & Café, in Corbin. The restaurant was a success and Sanders began to franchise his concept, Kentucky Fried Chicken (KFC). He began traveling across the country, visiting small towns and trying to convince restaurant owners to franchise his concept. Sanders would often cook meals for the restaurant owners, using his famous "secret recipe" of 11 herbs and spices.

In the 1940s, Sanders began to franchise his restaurant concept, Kentucky Fried Chicken (KFC). He sold the company in 1964 for $2 million. Sanders was also known for his distinctive appearance, always dressing in a white suit, white shirt, black string tie, and goatee. He also sported a white goatee and mustache, giving him a distinguished and recognizable look.

Despite selling the company, Sanders remained the public face of KFC and continued to travel and make appearances on behalf of the company. He even starred in a series of KFC commercials, where he would often be seen cooking and promoting the company's food. Sanders was also known for his philanthropy, often donating money and resources to various charitable causes.

On December 16, 1980, Sanders died at the age of 90. His legacy lives on, not only through the delicious KFC food that continues to be enjoyed by millions of people around the world, but also through the many charitable causes that he supported during his lifetime. Sanders was a true American icon and his story is one of hard work, determination, and the pursuit of the American dream.

In conclusion, Colonel Harland Sanders was more than just the man behind the famous KFC brand. He was a hardworking and determined individual who had a strong passion for cooking, and turned his love of cooking into a successful business empire. He was also a true American icon who was recognized and loved by many, not just for his delicious food but also for his philanthropy and dedication to making the world a better place. Sanders' legacy lives on and his story will continue to inspire many generations to come.

NEGATIVITY

Being surrounded by negative people can be an obstacle to success in several ways:

- Negative attitudes and beliefs can be contagious and can bring down the overall energy and morale of a team or group. This can lead to demotivation, lack of productivity, and poor performance.
- Negative people may discourage and discourage others from pursuing their goals and dreams, making it difficult for them to achieve success. They may also be critical and dismissive of new ideas and opportunities, which can stifle creativity and innovation.
- Negative people may also be less supportive and less likely to help others. This can make it harder for individuals to build networks, find mentors, and gain access to new opportunities.
- Negative people may also be more likely to engage in gossip and backbiting, which can lead to a toxic work environment and negatively affect employee morale and productivity.
- Negative people can also be draining and can take a toll on one's mental and emotional well-being, which

can affect overall health and well-being. This can have a negative impact on one's ability to perform at their best, focus and make good decisions.

In order to achieve success, it's important to surround yourself with people who are supportive, positive, and encouraging. It's also important to be selective about the influences in your life, and to distance yourself from people who are negative, critical, or toxic.

J K ROWLING

"You will never truly know yourself, or the strength of your relationships, until both have been tested by adversity."

— J.K. Rowling

Joanne Rowling, better known by her pen name J.K. Rowling, is a British author and philanthropist. She is best known for writing the Harry Potter series, which has become one of the best-selling book series in history. The books have been adapted into a successful film series, and have been translated into over 80 languages. The success of the Harry Potter series has made Rowling one of the wealthiest authors in the world, and she has used her wealth to support various charitable causes.

J K Rowling in 2010

Rowling was born in July 1965 in Yate, Gloucestershire, England. She attended Exeter University, where she studied French and Classics. After graduation, she worked as a researcher and bilingual secretary for Amnesty International, and later as a researcher for the Manchester Chamber of Commerce. In 1995, she married Jorge Arantes, with whom she had a daughter, Jessica Isabel Rowling Arantes. The couple divorced in 1999. In 2001, she married Neil Murray. They have two children together, David and Mackenzie.

Rowling began writing the Harry Potter series in the mid-1990s, while she was a single mother living on welfare in Edinburgh, Scotland. The idea for the series came to her while she was on a train ride from Manchester to London. The first book, Harry Potter and the Philosopher's Stone, was published in 1997 under the pseudonym "J.K." Rowling, the "K" standing for "Kathleen", her paternal grandmother's name. The book was an instant success, and six sequels followed, concluding with Harry Potter and the Deathly Hallows in 2007. The series has sold over 500 million copies worldwide and has been translated into over 80 languages.

The Harry Potter series has become a cultural phenomenon, with a devoted fan base known as "Potterheads". The books have been adapted into a successful film series, directed by David Yates and produced by David Heyman. The films have grossed over $7.7 billion worldwide, making it the highest-grossing film series of all time.

Rowling has received numerous awards for her work, including the British Book Award for Children's Book of the Year, the Whitbread Children's Book of the Year, the Hugo Award for Best Novel, the Bram Stoker Award for Best Work for Children, and the Locus Award for Best Fantasy Novel. She was also awarded an OBE (Officer of the Order of the British Empire) in 2001 and a CBE (Commander of the Order of the British Empire) in 2017 for services to literature and philanthropy.

In addition to her writing, Rowling is also known for her philanthropic work. She has supported multiple charities, including Comic Relief, Multiple Sclerosis Society of Great Britain, and One Parent Families. She has also set up her own charity, the Volant Charitable Trust, which aims to alleviate poverty and social inequality. In 2010, she was appointed a trustee of the National Literacy Trust, and in 2012, she was appointed as a Founding Trustee of The Volant Charitable Trust.

Rowling has also been a vocal advocate for multiple causes, including women's rights and LGBT rights. In 2014, she publicly supported the campaign for Scottish independence, and in 2016, she supported the campaign for the United Kingdom to remain in the European Union.

J.K. Rowling's story is one of perseverance and determination. Despite facing obstacles and negativity, she was able to achieve success and become one of the most successful authors of her time. She has also used her success to support multiple charitable causes and been vocal advocate for multiple causes, demonstrating that success can also be used for greater good. The Harry Potter series has become a cultural phenomenon, capturing the hearts of readers.

J.K. Rowling has spoken about how she struggled with depression and negative influences in her life before finding success as an author. She has credited much of her success to her ability to surround herself with positive people and to focus on her writing, despite the naysayers.

OPRAH WINFREY

"Surround yourself with only people who are going to lift you higher."

— Oprah Winfrey

Oprah Winfrey in 2014

Oprah Winfrey is a media mogul, philanthropist, and one of the most influential and successful women in the world. Born on January 29, 1954 in Kosciusko, Mississippi, Winfrey grew up in poverty and faced many challenges during her childhood. Despite this, she was an excellent student and was heavily involved in her church and community.

After graduating high school, Winfrey attended Tennessee State University, where she studied communication. It was during her college years that Winfrey began her career in media, working as a news anchor and television host in Nashville and Baltimore.

In 1983, Winfrey moved to Chicago to host a morning talk show called AM Chicago. The show was a huge success and its popularity quickly spread, leading to it being renamed The Oprah Winfrey Show. The show ran for 25 years and won multiple awards, including numerous Emmys. It was during her time on the show that Winfrey became one of the most influential and powerful women in the world.

Winfrey used her platform to tackle a wide range of topics, including social issues, personal development, and pop culture. She also interviewed a wide range of guests, from celebrities to politicians to everyday people. Her ability to connect with her audience and her willingness to share her own personal struggles made her relatable and helped to earn her a devoted following.

In addition to her daytime talk show, Winfrey also established a successful career as an actress and producer. She starred in a number of films, including "The Color Purple" and "Beloved", and produced several successful television shows, including "Dr. Phil" and "The Dr. Oz Show".

Winfrey is also known for her philanthropy and charitable work. She has established a number of foundations, including the Oprah Winfrey Leadership Academy for Girls in South Africa and the Oprah Winfrey Operating Foundation, which provides funding for a variety of causes and organizations. Winfrey has also donated millions of dollars to various charitable causes, including education and disaster relief.

Winfrey's impact on the entertainment industry and on popular culture is undeniable. She has broken barriers and shattered stereotypes, proving that women can have a powerful and influential voice in the media. Her ability to connect with her audience and her willingness to share her own personal struggles has made her relatable and helped to earn her a devoted following.

Oprah Winfrey is an inspiration to many, proving that with hard work and determination, anyone can achieve their dreams. On many occasions, Oprah has spoken publicly about the importance of surrounding yourself with positive people and cutting out negative influences in order to achieve success. She has credited much of her success to her ability to surround herself with a supportive team and to be selective about the people she allows into her inner circle.

ELON MUSK

"Pay attention to negative feedback, and solicit it, particularly from friends."

— Elon Musk

Elon Musk has become the most known yet controversial public figure who inspires, disrupts and persists on changing the status-quo. With quirky attitude, Elon Musk's popularity is both boon and bane for his investors. He, unlike many, seeks negativity and thrives on it by working his way out to improve better.

Elon Musk in 2018

Elon Musk is a South African-born American entrepreneur and businessman. He is the founder, CEO, and chief engineer/designer of SpaceX; early investor, CEO, and product architect of Tesla, Inc.; founder of The Boring Company; and co-founder of Neuralink. He was also co-founder and initial co-chairman of OpenAI. A centibillionaire, Musk is one of the richest people in the world.

Musk was born in Pretoria, South Africa, in 1971. He attended Pretoria Boys High School and then moved to

Canada aged 17 to attend Queen's University. He transferred to the University of Pennsylvania two years later, where he received dual bachelor's degrees in economics and physics. He moved on to Stanford University in 1995 to pursue a PhD in energy physics but decided instead to pursue a business career, co-founding web software company Zip2 with his brother, which was acquired by Compaq for $307 million in 1999.

Musk founded X.com, an online payment company, in 1999. The company merged with Confinity in 2000 to form the company that would eventually become PayPal, which was bought by eBay for $1.5 billion in October 2002. Musk founded SpaceX in 2002 with the goal of reducing space transportation costs in order to make space exploration more accessible. SpaceX has since developed the Falcon 1 and Falcon 9 launch vehicles, both designed to be reusable. In 2008, SpaceX became the first privately-funded company to send a spacecraft to the International Space Station.

In 2004, Musk joined Tesla, Inc., an electric vehicle manufacturer, as chairman and product architect. He helped create the company's first car, the Roadster, and became CEO in 2008. Under his leadership, the company has been at the forefront of the electric vehicle market, with its Model S, Model X, and Model 3 cars receiving widespread acclaim. In addition to his work at Tesla, Musk has also proposed the Hyperloop, a high-speed vactrain transportation system, and has invested in SolarCity, a solar energy services company.

In 2016, Musk founded The Boring Company, which aims to reduce traffic congestion by constructing underground tunnels for cars and high-speed transportation. In 2017, he co-founded Neuralink, a neurotechnology company focused on developing brain–computer interfaces, and founded The Boring Company, which aims to reduce traffic congestion through the construction of underground tunnels. He is also a co-founder and initial co-chairman of OpenAI, a nonprofit research company that aims to promote friendly AI in order to benefit humanity as a whole.

Musk's various business ventures have earned him a significant personal fortune, and he is considered one of the richest people in the world. He is also known for his ambitious goals and bold statements, including plans to send humans to Mars and his belief in the potential for artificial intelligence to surpass human intelligence.

Musk has been the subject of controversy, particularly in relation to his management style and his tendency to make bold and sometimes unrealistic statements. He has been criticized for his treatment of employees and for his public statements on a variety of topics. However, he has also been praised for his bold vision and for his efforts to promote sustainable energy and space exploration.

In summary, Elon Musk is a visionary entrepreneur, who through his various companies, has been at the forefront of the electric vehicle market, space exploration, tunneling, and brain-computer interfaces. He has a reputation for ambitious goals and bold statements, and is considered one of the richest people in the world. Despite the criticism he has faced, he is widely respected for his efforts to promote sustainable energy and space exploration and his contributions to technology and innovation.

Known for his ambitious projects, Elon Musk also had to face many nay-sayers and negative people, but he moved away from them and focused on his goals and vision. He has surrounded himself with talented and dedicated team members and has been able to achieve success in multiple industries such as electric cars, solar energy, and space exploration.

CHAPTER FOUR

DISCRIMINATION

Discrimination can be an obstacle to success in a number of ways.

Firstly, it can limit access to resources and opportunities. For example, people from marginalized groups may face discrimination in the job market, making it harder for them to find employment or advance in their careers. Similarly, discrimination in housing, education, and healthcare can make it difficult for individuals to access the resources they need to achieve their goals.

Secondly, discrimination can create a toxic work environment. People who face discrimination may feel isolated, demotivated and even depressed which can lead to decreased productivity, job dissatisfaction and possibly lead to them leaving the job or the industry.

Thirdly, discrimination can cause psychological harm. People who experience discrimination may internalize the negative messages they receive, leading to feelings of low self-worth and self-doubt. This can make it difficult for them to believe in their abilities and make it harder for them to achieve their goals.

Lastly, discrimination can lead to a lack of diversity in the workplace and in the society, which can negatively impact the creativity and innovation of the organization and the society as a whole.

Overall, discrimination can create a number of barriers to success for individuals and communities, making it difficult for them to reach their full potential. But successful people break the barriers in any form. The following real life examples are exactly who you want to look upto.

RUTH BADER GINSBURG

"Fight for the things that you care about, but do it in a way that will lead others to join you."

— Ruth Bader Ginsburg

Ruth Bader Ginsburg was an Associate Justice of the Supreme Court of the United States from 1993 until her death in 2020. She was appointed by President Bill Clinton and was the second woman to serve on the Supreme Court. Ginsburg's legal career spanned several decades and she was widely regarded as a feminist icon and a trailblazer for women's rights.

Ginsburg was born in Brooklyn, New York in 1933 and graduated from Cornell University in 1954. She then attended Harvard Law School, where she was one of only nine women in a class of over 500 students. Despite facing discrimination, Ginsburg excelled in her studies and graduated tied for first in her class.

Ruth Bader Ginsburg in 2016

After completing her education, Ginsburg faced difficulty finding a job due to her gender. She worked as a clerk for a federal judge and later as a professor at Rutgers University School of Law. In the 1970s, Ginsburg became involved in the women's rights movement and co-founded the Women's Rights Project at the American Civil Liberties Union (ACLU).

Ginsburg's work with the ACLU led to several important Supreme Court cases involving gender discrimination. In Reed v. Reed (1971), Ginsburg successfully argued that an Idaho law giving preference to men as administrators of estates was unconstitutional. In Frontiero v. Richardson (1973), Ginsburg successfully argued that a federal law allowing men to claim their wives as dependents for benefits but not allowing women to claim their husbands as dependents was discriminatory.

In 1980, President Jimmy Carter appointed Ginsburg to the United States Court of Appeals for the District of Columbia Circuit. She served in this position for thirteen years before being nominated to the Supreme Court by President Bill Clinton in 1993.

As a Supreme Court justice, Ginsburg was known for her dissenting opinions and for her support of progressive causes. She was a strong advocate for women's rights, voting to strike down abortion restrictions and voting in favor of affirmative action programs. She was also a strong advocate for LGBTQ rights and voted to strike down the Defense of Marriage Act in 2013.

Ginsburg's legal career and her contributions to the Supreme Court were widely recognized and she received numerous awards and honors. She was also known for her work ethic and her dedication to the law, even continuing to work while undergoing chemotherapy for cancer.

Ginsburg died on September 18, 2020 at the age of 87. Her death was widely mourned and her legacy is celebrated as an advocate for women's rights and as a trailblazer for gender equality.

Despite the discrimination and challenges throughout her career, her hard work, determination and her unwavering commitment to justice, helped her to become one of the most respected and influential figures in the legal world. Her legacy lives on and continues to inspire many generations to come.

MALALA YOUSAFZAI

"We realize the importance of our voices only when we are silenced."

— Malala Yousafzai

Malala Yousafzai in 2019

Malala Yousufzai is a Pakistani activist for female education and the youngest Nobel Prize laureate. Born on

July 12, 1997, in Mingora, Pakistan, Malala grew up in a time when the Taliban controlled her hometown and banned girls from attending school. Despite this, Malala's father, a school owner, was determined to provide education for his daughter and her brothers. Malala was educated at home and she also attended her father's school.

Malala's passion for education and her desire to speak out against the Taliban's oppression of women and girls led her to begin writing a blog for the BBC under a pseudonym in 2009. In the blog, she described her daily life, the challenges she faced, and her desire for an education.

In 2012, the Taliban targeted Malala specifically, shooting her in the head while she was on her way home from school. Miraculously, Malala survived and was taken to the United Kingdom for medical treatment. After her recovery, Malala continued to speak out about the importance of education for girls and the dangers posed by the Taliban.

In 2013, Malala was awarded Pakistan's National Youth Peace Prize and was nominated for the International Children's Peace Prize. She was also included in Time magazine's list of the 100 most influential people in the world.

In 2014, Malala and her family moved to the UK, where she continued her activism and education. She studied at Oxford University and became a UN Messenger of Peace in 2017. Malala also founded the Malala Fund, an organization that works to ensure that girls have the opportunity to attend school and receive a quality education.

Malala's activism and efforts have brought international attention to the plight of girls in Pakistan and around the world who are denied an education. Her advocacy has led to the enrollment of millions of girls in schools and her efforts continue to inspire many young people to speak out and take action for their rights.

In 2014, Malala Yousafzai was awarded the Nobel Peace Prize for her work in promoting girls' education and rights. At the age of 17, she became the youngest Nobel laureate in history.

Malala continues to speak out on issues of education and women's rights and is an inspiration to many young people around the world. She is a powerful voice for change and her story is a testament to the resilience, courage, and determination of young people to make a difference in the world.

In conclusion, Malala Yousufzai is an inspiration to many, a young girl who stood up against the Taliban and fought for the right of education for girls, even in the face of violence. Her courage and determination have brought international attention to the plight of girls denied an education, and her efforts have led to the enrollment of millions of girls in schools around the world. Malala is a reminder of the power of one person's voice to make a difference, and her story continues to inspire many young people to speak out and take action for their rights.

FRIDA KAHLO

"At the end of the day, we can endure much more than we think we can."

— Frida Kahlo

Frida Kahlo in 1932

Frida Kahlo was a Mexican painter who is considered one of the most important artists of the 20th century. She is best known for her self-portraits which often depicted her physical and emotional pain. Her work has been celebrated for its vivid colors, striking imagery and its ability to convey deep emotion.

Frida was born on July 6, 1907 in Coyoacán, Mexico City. She was the third of four children in a family of German and Mexican heritage. Frida was a sickly child and was bedridden for several months with polio at the age of six. She later recovered but suffered from chronic pain for the rest of her life.

Herpassion for art began at a young age. She was encouraged by her father, a photographer, who recognized her talent and provided her with art supplies. Frida began drawing and painting as a way to pass the time while she was bedridden.

In 1922, Frida's life changed dramatically when she was involved in a bus accident. She was impaled by a metal pole which caused injuries to her spine, pelvis and legs. The accident left her in chronic pain and she was bedridden for several months. It was during this time that Frida began to paint in earnest.

Frida's early paintings were primarily self-portraits. Her work was heavily influenced by her physical and emotional pain and her struggle to come to terms with her accident. Her paintings were often surreal, depicting distorted images of her own body.

In 1929, Frida met Diego Rivera, a renowned Mexican muralist and a leader of the Mexican muralism movement. They were married the following year and remained together until 1940. Frida's marriage to Rivera was tumultuous and the couple had several affairs during their marriage.

Despite the challenges in her personal life, Frida continued to paint. Her work was heavily influenced by Mexican folk art and the indigenous cultures of Mexico. She used bright colors, bold lines and striking imagery to convey her emotions and experiences.

All her work was not widely recognized during her lifetime. She had her first solo exhibition in Mexico in 1953, but it was not well received. Her work was seen as too radical and too personal. It wasn't until the 1970s that her work began to be recognized and celebrated.

Frida's work has been celebrated for its ability to convey deep emotion and its strong connection to Mexican culture and history. Her self-portraits are considered some of the most powerful and intimate paintings of the 20th century.

Frida's life was filled with physical and emotional pain, but she channeled that pain into her art. Her paintings are a reflection of her struggles and her resilience. She was a trailblazer for women in the art world, and her work has inspired generations of artists.

Frida's legacy has also been celebrated in popular culture. She has been the subject of several films, books and plays, and her work has been exhibited in galleries and museums all over the world. Her life and work have also been celebrated in Mexico, where she is considered a national treasure.

In conclusion, Frida Kahlo was a pioneering artist who overcame significant obstacles to become one of the most important artists of the 20th century. Her work, heavily influenced by her physical and emotional pain, has been celebrated for its ability to convey deep emotion and its strong connection to Mexican culture and history. Her legacy continues to inspire generations of artists, and her paintings remain a powerful reflection of her struggles and resilience.

CHAPTER FIVE

ACCIDENT

Accidents can be significant obstacles to success because they can cause physical or psychological injuries that can limit an individual's ability to function normally. For example, an accident that results in a physical injury can limit an individual's mobility, strength, and endurance, making it difficult to perform tasks that were once routine. Accidents can also cause emotional trauma, such as depression, anxiety, or post-traumatic stress disorder, which can negatively impact an individual's motivation, focus, and decision-making abilities.

Additionally, accidents can result in financial difficulties, as they can lead to expensive medical bills and lost wages. This can cause stress and make it difficult for the person to focus on their work or personal goals. Furthermore, accidents can also cause a loss of confidence, self-esteem, and self-worth, which can be detrimental to one's self-motivation and can discourage them from pursuing their goals. But resilient people overcome the horrible incidents with flying colors.

BEAR GRYLLS

"You can't become a decent horseman until you fall off and get up again, a good number of times. There's life in a nutshell."

— Bear Grylls

Bear Grylls in 2012

Bear Grylls is a British adventurer, author, and television presenter, best known for his survival and outdoor adventure series, Man vs. Wild. Born on June 7, 1974, in London, England, Grylls grew up with a love for the outdoors and adventure.

Grylls' career began in the British Army, where he served in the 21 SAS (Special Air Service) for three years. After leaving the army, he began a career as an adventurer and mountaineer.

He survived a serious paragliding accident in 1996. Grylls was paragliding in the Welsh mountains when his parachute malfunctioned, causing him to crash to the ground. The accident left him with multiple broken bones, including a broken back, and a collapsed lung. He was in a coma for several days and required extensive rehabilitation to recover. In 1998, he became the youngest British climber to reach the summit of Mount Everest at the age of 23.

Grylls' first television series, Man vs. Wild, premiered in 2006 and quickly became a hit. The show followed Grylls as he was dropped off in remote locations around the world and had to survive and find his way back to civilization. The series ran for seven seasons and was broadcast in over 180 countries.

In addition to his television series, Grylls is also a bestselling author, with several books on survival and outdoor adventure. He has also served as a motivational speaker, sharing his experiences and lessons learned from his adventures with audiences around the world.

Grylls' outdoor and survival skills have been put to the test in some of the most extreme environments in the world, from the Arctic to the Sahara Desert. He has also participated in a number of high-profile stunts, such as a parachute jump into the Arctic and a climb to the summit of Mount Everest without supplemental oxygen.

His tactics and skills have not only been demonstrated on screen but also put into practice in real-life survival scenarios. He has been recognized by the British SAS for his ability to survive in the wilderness, and he has been awarded an honorary commission as a lieutenant commander in the Royal Navy for his promotion of the military.

Grylls is also known for his philanthropic work, he has been an ambassador for the Duke of Edinburgh Award, which encourages young people to participate in outdoor activities and he also established the Bear Grylls Survival Academy, which offers survival courses for both children and adults.

In conclusion, Bear Grylls is a well-known adventurer, author, and television presenter, who has become famous for his survival and outdoor adventure series, Man vs. Wild. He has demonstrated his survival skills in extreme environments, has been recognized for his ability to survive in the wilderness, and has been awarded an honorary commission as a lieutenant commander in the Royal Navy for his promotion of the military. He is also known for his philanthropic work, encouraging young people to participate in outdoor activities and offering survival courses for both children and adults. Grylls is a true inspiration to many, who has shown that with determination, hard work and a love for adventure, one can accomplish anything.

ARON RALSTON

"You'll never find your limits until you've gone too far."

— Aron Ralston

Aron Ralston in 2009

Aron Ralston is an American outdoorsman and motivational speaker who is known for surviving a harrowing accident in 2003. Ralston was on a solo hike in

Bluejohn Canyon, Utah when he was trapped by a dislodged boulder that had fallen on his arm, pinning him against the canyon wall. He was trapped for five days, during which time he was forced to ration his food and water and attempt to free himself by chipping away at the boulder with a dull multi-tool.

When all his efforts proved futile, Ralston realized that the only way to escape was to amputate his own arm. With a tourniquet made from his clothing, he broke the bones in his arm and cut through the muscle and tendons with the multi-tool, before finally freeing himself and hiking to safety.

Ralston's story of survival and determination has been widely reported in the media, and he has since used his experience to become an advocate for wilderness safety and to inspire others to overcome their own challenges.

Ralston's accident was a life-changing experience, and he has since become an advocate for wilderness safety, using his experience to help others. He wrote a bestselling book, "Between a Rock and a Hard Place", detailing his experience, which was later made into a movie "127 Hours" by Danny Boyle. He also created a website, AronRalston.org, which provides information on wilderness survival and encourages others to share their own survival stories.

His determination to survive and overcome the challenges he faced has been an inspiration to many. His story is a powerful reminder of the human spirit's ability to endure and overcome even the most difficult of situations. He has shown that with determination, willpower, and the ability to think outside the box, it's possible to achieve the impossible.

Ralston has also been a guest speaker at numerous events, sharing his story and inspiring others to overcome their own challenges. He has been invited to speak at schools, corporations, and other organizations, and he has been recognized by many for his strength and determination.

In addition to his work as a motivational speaker, Ralston has also continued to pursue his love of the outdoors. He has climbed many of the most challenging peaks in the United States and has also completed several endurance events such as marathons, triathlons, and Ironman competitions.

Despite the accident, Ralston has not let it slow him down or limit his ability to achieve his goals. He has continued to challenge himself and has become an inspiration to many. He is a testament to the human spirit's ability to endure and overcome even the most difficult of circumstances.

In conclusion, Aron Ralston's story of survival and determination is an inspiration to many. His experience serves as a powerful reminder of the human spirit's ability to endure and overcome even the most difficult of situations. He has shown that with determination, willpower, and the ability to think outside the box, it's possible to achieve the impossible. He has also become an advocate for wilderness safety, using his experience to help others and continues to inspire many as a motivational speaker.

JAMES CLEAR

"You do not rise to the level of your goals. You fall to the level of your systems."

— James Clear

James Clear in 2014

James Clear is an American author, speaker and productivity expert, known for his work on habits and behavior change. He is the author of the bestselling book

"Atomic Habits: An Easy & Proven Way to Build Good Habits & Break Bad Ones" and his work has been featured in numerous publications including The New York Times, Time, and Entrepreneur.

Clear was born on November 2, 1983, in the United States, and grew up in a small town in Ohio. He attended Miami University in Ohio, where he studied economics and psychology. After graduation, Clear began working in various jobs, including as a personal trainer, a wedding photographer, and a software developer.

Clear was involved in an accident when he was a teenager, which left him with a traumatic brain injury. The accident caused him to struggle with memory loss, attention deficits, and other cognitive challenges for many years. With sheer resilience and brilliant attitude, he overcame the traumatic accident.

In 2010, Clear began experimenting with habit formation and began writing about his experiences on his personal blog. He quickly gained a following, and his writing on the topic of habits and behavior change quickly became popular.

In 2012, Clear published his first book, "Making Habits, Breaking Habits: Why We Do Things, Why We Don't, and How to Make Any Change Stick". The book explores the science behind habit formation and provides practical strategies for making lasting change.

His effort has been widely recognized, and he has been invited to speak on the topic of habits and behavior change at conferences and events around the world. He has also been featured in numerous publications, including The New York Times, Time, and Entrepreneur.

Clear's work on habits is based on the idea that small, consistent actions are the key to achieving long-term goals.

He emphasizes the importance of breaking down large goals into small, manageable tasks and focusing on progress over perfection. He also encourages readers to focus on the process of building habits rather than the outcome, and to use systems and structures to support habit formation.

Clear's message resonates with many people, and he has a large following on social media and a popular newsletter. He also runs a popular online course, which teaches people how to build better habits and achieve their goals.

In addition to his work on habits, Clear is also an advocate for the use of technology to support productivity and goal-setting. He promotes the use of apps, tools, and other technology to help people stay organized and focused on their goals.

In conclusion, James Clear is an author, speaker and productivity expert, who is widely recognized for his work on habits and behavior change. He has published several books on the topic and his work has been featured in numerous publications. Clear's work is based on the idea that small, consistent actions are the key to achieving long-term goals and he emphasizes the importance of breaking down large goals into small, manageable tasks and focusing on progress over perfection. He has a large following on social media and a popular newsletter, his message resonates with many people and he continues to inspire others to build better habits and achieve their goals.

CHAPTER SIX

FAILURE

Failure can be an obstacle to success, but it can also be a valuable learning experience. Failure can teach valuable lessons, such as persistence, determination, and resilience. It can also help individuals learn from their mistakes and make adjustments to their strategies in order to achieve success in the future. Many successful people attribute their success to the failures they've experienced and the lessons they've learned from them. Failure can also be a humbling experience and can help individuals gain a better perspective on what's truly important in life.

Overcoming failures is important to succeed because it helps individuals develop a growth mindset, which is the belief that abilities and intelligence can be developed through effort and learning. When people overcome failure, they learn that setbacks are not permanent and that they can bounce back from them. This belief in one's own ability to improve helps individuals to persevere through difficult times and to keep working towards their goals even when faced with obstacles.

Another way that overcoming failures is important for success is that it can help individuals learn from their mistakes. Failure can provide valuable feedback and insight into what didn't work and what needs to be done differently in order to achieve success in the future. Failure can also help individuals identify their weaknesses and areas where they need to improve, which is essential for personal and professional growth.

Additionally, overcoming failures can build resilience, which is the ability to bounce back from adversity. Resilience is a critical trait for success, as it allows individuals to handle stress and pressure effectively and to adapt to changing circumstances. People who have overcome failures are often better equipped to handle future challenges and to persevere in the face of adversity.

Overall, overcoming failures is important for success because it helps individuals develop a growth mindset, learn from mistakes, and build resilience which are all essential traits for achieving success in life.

DONALD TRUMP

"What separates the winners from the losers is how a person reacts to each new twist of fate."

— Donald J. Trump

Donald J. Trump is a businessman and politician who served as the 45th President of the United States from January 20, 2017 to January 20, 2021. He is the first president in U.S. history to have been impeached twice by the House of Representatives.

Donald J. Trump in 2017

Before entering politics, Trump was a successful businessman and real estate developer. He is the chairman and president of The Trump Organization, a U.S.-based real-estate developer, and the founder of Trump Entertainment Resorts, which operates numerous casinos and hotels across the world. He is also the founder of Trump Foundation, a charitable foundation which has donated millions of dollars to veterans and other charitable causes.

Trump first gained national attention in the 1970s and 1980s as a New York City real estate developer, particularly for his redevelopment of the Grand Hyatt hotel in Manhattan and the construction of Trump Tower. He later expanded his business to include Atlantic City casinos, golf courses, and hotels. Trump's brand of luxury real estate and his outspoken, brash public persona helped to make him one of the most well-known and recognizable figures in American business.

In 2015, Trump announced his candidacy for President of the United States in the 2016 election, running on a platform of economic nationalism and "Make America Great Again." He campaigned as an outsider, criticizing the political establishment and promising to bring jobs back to the country, secure the borders, and "drain the swamp" in Washington. Despite being considered a long shot by many political analysts, Trump won the Republican nomination and eventually defeated Democratic nominee Hillary Clinton in the general election.

As President, Trump implemented a number of policies that aimed to revitalize the economy, create jobs, and boost national security. He implemented tax cuts, rolled back regulations, and renegotiated trade deals, which led to a period of economic growth. He also implemented a hardline immigration policy, which included a controversial travel ban and the construction of a border wall with Mexico.

Trump's presidency was also marked by a number of controversies and divisive actions. He was widely criticized for his handling of the COVID-19 pandemic, particularly for downplaying the threat of the virus and for failing to take adequate measures to slow its spread. He also faced widespread criticism for his handling of racial tensions and civil unrest, particularly in the wake of the death of George Floyd.

Trump's presidency was also marked by numerous investigations and impeachment proceedings. In 2019, the House of Representatives launched an impeachment inquiry into Trump over his attempts to pressure Ukraine to investigate Joe Biden, his political rival. He was subsequently impeached by the House on two articles of impeachment: abuse of power and obstruction of Congress. He was acquitted by the Senate on both charges.

On Jan 6, 2021, Trump supporters who believed the 2020 presidential election was rigged, stormed the U.S Capitol building, interrupting the certification of the 2020 presidential election results by Congress. This led to a second impeachment by the House on the charge of incitement of insurrection. Trump was acquitted by the Senate again.

Donald J. Trump has had a number of failures throughout his life, both in business and in politics. Here are a few examples:

- Atlantic City Casinos: In the 1990s, Trump invested heavily in Atlantic City's casino industry, buying and building several properties. However, several of these casinos, including the Trump Taj Mahal, filed for bankruptcy multiple times. He eventually sold or closed most of his Atlantic City properties, resulting in significant financial losses.
- Trump University: In 2005, Trump launched Trump University, a for-profit education company that offered courses in real estate and entrepreneurship. However, the university faced multiple lawsuits and investigations, with many students alleging that the

program was a scam and that they had not received the education they were promised. Trump settled the lawsuits for $25 million shortly before taking office as president.

- Trump Steaks: In 2007, Trump launched a line of premium steaks, which were sold through The Sharper Image and other retailers. However, the steaks received poor reviews and the line was quickly discontinued.
- Trump Network: In 2009, Trump launched a multi-level marketing company called Trump Network, which sold a line of health and wellness products. However, the company faced multiple lawsuits and struggled to attract customers, ultimately shutting down in 2012.
- 2016 Presidential Campaign: Trump had made attempts to run for president in the past, however in 2016 he announced his candidacy for the republican nomination, during the campaign he faced many controversies like the Access Hollywood tape, where he was caught on tape making lewd comments about women. Despite many people thinking he wouldn't win, he eventually won the republican nomination but lost the general election to Hillary Clinton.
- Impeachment proceedings: Trump faced two impeachment proceedings during his presidency. The first impeachment was related to his attempts to pressure Ukraine to investigate Joe Biden, his political rival. The second impeachment was related to his role in inciting the Capitol riots on January 6, 2021, which interrupted the certification of the 2020 presidential election results by Congress. He was acquitted by the Senate on both charges.
- 2020 Presidential Election: Trump lost the 2020 Presidential election to Joe Biden, and despite his claims

of widespread voter fraud, his campaign legal team failed to provide any evidence to support these claims, and the election was certified by Congress.

These are just a few examples of the many failures that Trump has experienced throughout his life. Despite these setbacks, he has been able to bounce back and continue to be a successful businessman and influential political figure.

WALT DISNEY

"I dream, I test my dreams against my beliefs, I dare to take risks, and I execute my vision to make those dreams come true."

— Walt Disney

Walt Disney was a visionary animator, film producer, and entrepreneur who created some of the most beloved characters and stories in the world. Born on December 5, 1901, in Chicago, Illinois, Disney had a passion for art and animation from a young age. He began his career as a cartoonist and eventually started his own animation studio, The Walt Disney Company.

Walt Disney in 1946

Walt Disney, despite his many successes, also had his share of failures and setbacks throughout his career. Some of the notable failures in his life include:

- The failure of Disney's first animation studio: In the 1920s, Disney started his first animation studio, called Laugh-O-Gram Studio, in Kansas City. The studio struggled financially and eventually went bankrupt, forcing Disney to move to Hollywood in search of new opportunities.

- The loss of the Oswald the Lucky Rabbit character: In 1927, Disney created the character Oswald the Lucky Rabbit, which was a huge success. However, due to a legal dispute with the distributor, Disney lost the rights to Oswald and had to come up with a new character, which led to the creation of Mickey Mouse.
- The failure of "The Sorcerer's Apprentice" segment of "Fantasia": The segment was a massive budget and technical failure for the studio, as well as being a commercial failure upon its initial release, it was only after the re-release of the film that the segment became one of the most popular segments.
- The failure of Disney's first live-action feature film: In 1950, Disney released his first live-action feature film, "Treasure Island". The film was a commercial failure and resulted in significant financial losses for the studio.
- The failure of "America the Beautiful" and "EPCOT Center": Disney's ambitious plans to build an experimental city, "EPCOT Center" (Experimental Prototype Community of Tomorrow) and the "America the Beautiful" pavilion at Disneyland were both failures as they never materialized after Walt Disney's death.
- The failure of "The Black Cauldron": In 1985, Disney released "The Black Cauldron", an animated fantasy film based on a series of Welsh myths. The film was a commercial and critical failure, resulting in significant financial losses for the studio.

Despite these failures, Walt Disney's vision, creativity, and determination helped him overcome these setbacks and continue to create some of the most beloved characters and stories in the world. He remains an inspiration to many people and his legacy continues to be celebrated today.

Disney's first major success was the creation of the character Oswald the Lucky Rabbit in 1927. However, due to a legal dispute with the distributor, Disney lost the rights to Oswald and had to come up with a new character. This led to the creation of Mickey Mouse, who made his debut in the 1928 short film "Steamboat Willie". Mickey Mouse quickly became a cultural icon and Disney's studio went on to produce a number of other successful cartoon characters such as Donald Duck, Goofy, and Pluto.

In addition to animation, Disney also had a passion for filmmaking and storytelling. In 1937, Disney released its first full-length animated film, "Snow White and the Seven Dwarfs", which was a critical and commercial success. Disney's studio went on to produce a number of other successful animated films, including "Fantasia", "Dumbo", "Cinderella", "Sleeping Beauty", and "The Little Mermaid".

Disney was also an innovator and pioneer in the theme park industry. In 1955, he opened Disneyland in Anaheim, California, the first of its kind, and the park immediately became one of the most popular tourist destinations in the world.

HENRY FORD

"Whether you think you can, or you think you can't—you're right."

— Henry Ford

Henry Ford in 1919

Henry Ford was an American industrialist, businessman, and inventor who is best known for founding the Ford Motor Company and for developing the assembly line technique of mass production. He was one of the most influential figures of the 20th century and his innovations had a significant impact on the American economy and society.

Ford was born in 1863 on a farm in what is now Dearborn, Michigan. He had a natural mechanical aptitude and began experimenting with internal combustion engines at an early age. He worked as a machinist and then as an engineer for a number of companies before starting his own business, the Detroit Automobile Company, in 1899. However, the company failed and he left in 1901 to start the Henry Ford Company, which later became the Cadillac Motor Company.

In 1903, Ford founded the Ford Motor Company and began manufacturing automobiles. He introduced the Model T in 1908, which was an affordable car that was built on an assembly line. The assembly line allowed Ford to produce cars much more efficiently and at a lower cost than before, making them accessible to a wider range of people. The Model T became one of the most popular cars in the world and Ford's assembly line technique revolutionized the automobile industry and changed the way goods were manufactured.

Ford's innovations extended beyond the assembly line. He also introduced the $5 workday, which doubled the typical factory worker's wages and reduced the workday from 9 hours to 8 hours. This helped to improve the standard of living for his workers and made it possible for them to afford the cars they were building. He also introduced the concept of the "Sociological Department", which aimed to improve the lives of his workers by providing them with better working conditions, health services and recreational activities.

During World War 1, Ford was a strong advocate for peace and helped to fund the American Peace Society. After the war, he continued to support peace initiatives and was a vocal critic of American involvement in World War II. Despite his anti-war stance, Ford's factories were used to produce war materials.

In the 1920s, Ford purchased a newspaper, The Dearborn Independent, which he used to publish anti-Semitic articles. He later apologized for the articles and closed the newspaper.

In the later years of his life, Ford became increasingly reclusive and handed over the management of the company to his grandson, Henry Ford II. He died in 1947 at the age of 84.

Ford's impact on the world was enormous. His innovations in production and labor practices led to the creation of the middle class, and his Model T changed the way people lived, worked and traveled. The assembly line technique that he developed is still used today in many industries, and his ideas on social responsibility and workers' rights continue to influence business practices.

Henry Ford, despite his many successes as an industrialist and inventor, also had his share of failures and setbacks throughout his career. Some of the notable failures in his life include:

- The failure of the Ford Motor Company: In 1903, Ford founded the Ford Motor Company, but the company struggled in its early years and almost went bankrupt in 1907.
- The failure of the Ford Model A: In 1903, Ford introduced the Model A, which was intended to replace the Model N. However, the Model A did not sell well and was quickly discontinued.
- The failure of the Ford Model K: In 1906, Ford introduced the Model K, which was intended to be a luxury car. However, the Model K was too expensive and did not sell well, and was discontinued after only two years in production.

- The failure of the Ford Model T: In 1908, Ford introduced the Model T, which was intended to be a car for the masses. However, the Model T was not well-received initially, and it took several years for it to become popular.
- The failure of the Ford Tri-Motor: In 1925, Ford introduced the Tri-Motor, which was intended to be a commercial airliner. However, the Tri-Motor was not very successful and was soon surpassed by more advanced aircraft.
- The failure of Fordlandia: In 1927, Ford acquired a large tract of land in the Amazon rainforest in Brazil, with the intent of creating a rubber plantation. However, the project was plagued by poor planning, mismanagement, and cultural misunderstandings, and it ultimately failed to produce the expected amount of rubber.

Despite these failures, Henry Ford's innovation and perseverance helped him to overcome these setbacks and continue to make significant contributions to the automobile industry. His development of the assembly line and use of interchangeable parts revolutionized manufacturing and made cars more affordable for the average person. He remains an inspiration to many people and his legacy continues to be celebrated today.

CHAPTER SEVEN

IMMIGRATION

Immigrating to a new country can certainly present many obstacles and challenges that can make it difficult to achieve success. These obstacles may include language barriers, cultural differences, lack of social connections, and difficulty finding employment or housing. However, many immigrants have been able to overcome these obstacles and achieve success in their new countries.

One way to overcome these obstacles is to learn the language of the new country as fluently as possible. This can help with communication and understanding the culture, making it easier to find employment and build connections. Additionally, seeking out resources and support within the immigrant community can be helpful. Many communities have organizations that provide assistance with finding employment, housing, and other services.

Another important aspect is to maintain a positive attitude, be persistent and determined. It is important to keep in mind that success is not always immediate, and it may take time and effort to achieve one's goals. Also, leveraging any existing skills, networks, and resources can be a valuable asset to overcome the obstacles.

In summary, while immigration can present many obstacles to success, many immigrants have been able to overcome them and achieve success in their new countries by learning the language, seeking out resources and support, and maintaining a positive attitude and persistence.

ARIANNA HUFFINGTON

"Fearlessness is not the absence of fear. It's the mastery of fear. It's about getting up one more time than we fall down."

— Arianna Huffington

Arianna Huffington is a Greek-American author, syndicated columnist, and businesswoman. She was born in Athens, Greece, in 1950 and immigrated to the United States in 1980. She is best known as the co-founder of The Huffington Post, a news and blog website that was launched in 2005.

Huffington began her career as a writer, authoring several books on political and cultural topics. She was also a regular guest on political talk shows, where she gained a reputation as a prominent conservative commentator. However, in the mid-2000s, she shifted her focus to the world of digital media and co-founded The Huffington Post with Ken Lerer and Jonah Peretti.

Arianna Huffington in 2011

The Huffington Post quickly became one of the most popular and influential news and opinion websites on the internet. It featured a mix of original content from Huffington and other prominent writers, as well as aggregation of news and opinion from other sources. The website also featured a large community of bloggers, who contributed content on a wide range of topics.

In 2011, The Huffington Post was acquired by AOL for $315 million, and Huffington became the President and Editor-in-Chief of The Huffington Post Media Group.

Under her leadership, the website continued to grow in popularity and influence, and it became one of the most widely read and respected sources of news and opinion on the internet.

In addition to her work with The Huffington Post, Huffington is also a prominent author and speaker. She has written several books, including "The Huffington Post Complete Guide to Blogging," "On Becoming Fearless," and "Thrive: The Third Metric to Redefining Success and Creating a Life of Well-Being, Wisdom, and Wonder." She has also been a keynote speaker at numerous conferences and events, where she has discussed topics such as digital media, entrepreneurship, and women in leadership.

Huffington is also a vocal advocate for a number of social and political issues. She is a strong supporter of women's rights and has been a vocal critic of the gender pay gap and other forms of discrimination against women. She has also been an advocate for a number of other causes, including education, healthcare, and the environment.

In 2016, Arianna stepped down as the Editor-in-Chief of Huffington Post to focus on her new venture, Thrive Global, a company focused on helping people improve their well-being and performance through corporate wellness programs, digital products and workshops, and other services.

After immigrating to the United States in 1980, Arianna Huffington faced several challenges as she built her career and established herself in her new country. Some of these challenges include:

- Language barriers: Huffington spoke Greek as her first language and had to learn English as a second language. This presented a challenge for her as she had to learn a new language in order to communicate effectively and establish herself in her new country.

- Cultural differences: Huffington had to adapt to a new culture and customs in the United States, which can be challenging for anyone who has immigrated. She had to learn about the American way of life and the cultural norms that are different from her home country.

- Building a professional network: Huffington had to start from scratch in building a professional network in the United States. This can be a daunting task for anyone who has immigrated, as it can be difficult to connect with people and find professional opportunities.

- Establishing credibility: Huffington was a relatively unknown figure in the United States when she first immigrated, and she had to work hard to establish credibility and build a reputation as a writer and commentator.

- Overcoming stereotypes: As a foreigner and a woman, Huffington faced the challenge of overcoming stereotypes and biases in her new country. Despite these challenges, she was able to establish herself as a successful journalist, author, and businesswoman.

Throughout her career, Arianna Huffington has been recognized for her contributions to the world of digital media and journalism. She has received numerous awards and honors, including an honorary degree from the New School in New York City, and the Matrix Award for her contributions to the world of new media.

VIKTOR FRANKL

"When we are no longer able to change a situation, we are challenged to change ourselves."

— Viktor E. Frankl

Viktor Frankl in 1965

Viktor Frankl was an Austrian neurologist, psychiatrist, and Holocaust survivor, who is best known for his book

"Man's Search for Meaning". Born on March 26, 1905, in Vienna, Austria, Frankl studied medicine and later specialized in neurology and psychiatry. He began his professional career as a psychiatrist and psychotherapist, but his life and work were forever changed by his experiences in Nazi concentration camps during World War II.

Frankl was arrested by the Nazis in 1942 and was subsequently sent to the Auschwitz concentration camp. He would go on to spend time in several other concentration camps, including Dachau and Türkheim. Despite the unimaginable horror and suffering he experienced, Frankl managed to find meaning and purpose in his ordeal, which he later described in his book "Man's Search for Meaning".

In the book, Frankl argues that the human search for meaning is the primary motivational force in life, and that even in the face of extreme suffering and adversity, it is possible to find meaning and purpose. He developed a therapeutic approach called logotherapy, which is based on the idea that the primary goal of therapy is to help individuals find meaning in their lives.

Frankl's book has become a classic and has been translated into over 30 languages. It has been widely read and has had a profound impact on the field of psychology and the understanding of the human experience.

After the end of World War II, Viktor Frankl immigrated to the United States where he faced several challenges in his personal and professional life. Some of the notable challenges he faced include:

- Language barrier: Frankl had to learn English in order to be able to communicate and work in the United States.

This was a difficult task as Frankl was already in his 40s and had spent most of his life speaking German.

- Professional recognition: Frankl had to establish himself as a reputable therapist and psychiatrist in the United States. This was a difficult task as he was an unknown figure in the American professional community and had to compete with established figures in the field.
- Cultural differences: Frankl had to adapt to the cultural differences between Austria and the United States, which included different attitudes towards therapy and mental health. He also had to navigate the different professional regulations and standards in the United States.
- Personal challenges: Frankl had to come to terms with the trauma and losses he had experienced during the Holocaust. He also had to adjust to living in a new country and being separated from his family and friends.

Despite these challenges, Frankl was able to establish himself as a reputable therapist and psychiatrist in the United States. He went on to write several more books, including "Man's Search for Ultimate Meaning" and "The Will to Meaning", which were well-received and helped to further establish his reputation. Frankl also continued to give lectures and workshops, and his logotherapy approach continues to be used by therapists and counselors today.

WANG YUNG-CHING

"It is easy for the frugal to become extravagant, but very difficult to reverse the process."

— Wang Yung-ching

Y C Wang in 1966

Wang Yung-ching (1917-2008) was a Taiwanese businessman and philanthropist. He was the founder and chairman of Formosa Plastics Group, one of the largest petrochemical companies in the world.

Wang was born in a small village in Taiwan and began working in his father's rice and sugarcane farm at a young age. Wang Yung-ching, also known as Y.C. Wang, immigrated to Taiwan from mainland China in 1949, after the Chinese Civil War. As a result of the war, the island of Taiwan was separated from the mainland and became the Republic of China, with a new government led by the Nationalist Party (Kuomintang).

One of the main challenges that Wang faced after immigrating to Taiwan was building a business from scratch in a new and unfamiliar environment. In the 1940s, he started a small plastics factory with a partner, which eventually grew into the Formosa Plastics Group. The company expanded rapidly and became a major player in the global petrochemical industry, with operations in Taiwan, the United States, and China. This included dealing with challenges like limited resources, lack of access to technology and expertise, and a lack of established business networks.

Another challenge that Wang faced was navigating the political and economic landscape of Taiwan during this time period. The country was under martial law from 1949 to 1987, which limited freedom of speech, the press, and assembly, and made it difficult for private businesses to operate. The government also had a strong influence on the economy and implemented policies that favored state-owned enterprises. Wang had to navigate these challenges and find ways to grow his business despite the limitations imposed by the government.

In addition, Wang also faced the challenges of being an immigrant in a new country. He had to adapt to a new culture, language, and way of life, while also trying to build a successful business. Despite these challenges, Wang was able to overcome them through his hard work and determination, which ultimately led to the success of the Formosa Plastics Group.

Wang was known for his frugality and hard work, and was highly respected by his employees. He was also a generous philanthropist, donating large sums of money to education and medical research.

Wang's philanthropic efforts focused on education and science, he believed that education and science have great power to change the world. He donated to many universities, research institutions and medical centers in Taiwan, Mainland China and United States. He also established a number of foundation to support the education and science.

Wang passed away in 2008, but his legacy lives on through the Formosa Plastics Group and the many charitable organizations he supported during his lifetime.

CHAPTER EIGHT

POVERTY

Poverty can be a significant obstacle to success as it often limits access to education, resources, and opportunities. However, there are several ways in which individuals can overcome poverty and achieve success:

- Education: Access to education is crucial for breaking the cycle of poverty. Education can open doors to better job opportunities and higher earning potential.
- Entrepreneurship: Starting a small business can be a way for individuals to create their own opportunities and generate income.
- Networking: Building relationships and networking with people who have the resources and connections to help can be beneficial.
- Access to resources: Having access to resources such as a reliable internet connection, transportation, and healthcare can help individuals overcome the challenges of poverty.
- Mentorship: Having a mentor who has experience and knowledge in a particular field can be a valuable resource for individuals trying to overcome poverty.

- Government policies: Government policies that support low-income families, such as affordable housing, food assistance, and healthcare, can help ease the burden of poverty.

It's important to note that overcoming poverty is not just an individual effort, systemic and structural changes are necessary to truly address poverty and provide equal opportunities for all.

MO IBRAHIM

"I think we need to look at ourselves first. We should practice what we're preaching. Otherwise, we are hypocrites."

— Mo Ibrahim

Mo Ibrahim is a Sudanese-British businessman, philanthropist, and advocate for good governance in Africa. He is the founder of the Mo Ibrahim Foundation, which is focused on promoting good governance and leadership on the African continent.

Born in a poor family from Sudan in 1946, Ibrahim with a tremendous hardwork, moved to the United Kingdom in the 1970s to study electrical engineering. After completing his education, he began a career in telecommunications, working for various companies in the United Kingdom and Europe before starting his own business. In 1998, he founded Celtel, a mobile phone company that operated in several African countries. Under his leadership, the company grew rapidly, and it was eventually sold for over $3 billion.

Mo Ibrahim in 2007

With his success in business, Ibrahim has become a leading philanthropist and advocate for good governance in Africa. In 2006, he founded the Mo Ibrahim Foundation, which is focused on promoting good governance and leadership on the African continent. The foundation has several initiatives including the Ibrahim Prize for Achievement in African Leadership, which is awarded to a former African head of state or government who has demonstrated exceptional leadership.

Ibrahim is also a strong advocate for the development of the telecommunications sector in Africa, as a means of promoting economic growth and development. He has been a vocal supporter of policies that promote competition and private investment in the sector, and he has worked to promote the use of mobile phones and other technologies to drive economic development in Africa.

In addition to his philanthropic work, Ibrahim has also been an active participant in various policy and advocacy groups, including the World Economic Forum, the Africa Progress Panel, and the African Union. He has also served as an advisor to several African leaders and governments on issues related to governance and development.

Ibrahim's work has been widely recognized, and he has received numerous awards and honors for his contributions to Africa's development. He has been honored by several African countries, including Sudan, Ghana, and Senegal, and he has received several international awards, including the Presidential Medal of Freedom from the United States.

Rising from an average household, Ibrahim self-made a legend setting an example for the entire African continent.

JACK MA

"*Today is difficult, tomorrow is much more difficult, but the day after tomorrow is beautiful. Most people die tomorrow evening.*"

— Jack Ma

Jack Ma in 2018

Jack Ma, also known as Ma Yun, is a Chinese businessman, philanthropist, and founder of the Alibaba Group, one of the world's largest e-commerce businesses. Born in Hangzhou, China in 1964, Ma grew up in a poor family and struggled academically as a child. Despite this, he developed a passion for English and teaching, which led him to become an English teacher after graduating from Hangzhou Teacher's Institute.

In 1995, while working as an English teacher, Ma became interested in the potential of the internet and decided to start his own business. He founded the Alibaba Group, an online marketplace connecting Chinese manufacturers with overseas buyers, in 1999. The company quickly grew in popularity and success, and by 2014, it had become the world's largest e-commerce company by gross merchandise volume.

Alibaba Group operates several platforms, including the Taobao Marketplace, the Tmall online retail platform, and the Alibaba.com wholesale platform. These platforms connect businesses and consumers from all over the world, allowing small and medium-sized enterprises to access global markets. Additionally, the Alibaba Group also operates several other businesses, including online and mobile payments, cloud computing, and a digital media and entertainment division.

Ma's success with Alibaba has also led him to become one of China's wealthiest and most influential businessmen. In addition to his business ventures, Ma is also known for his philanthropic efforts. He established the Jack Ma Foundation in 2014, which focuses on education, environmental protection, and public health. The foundation has also been involved in disaster relief efforts, such as providing aid to the victims of the 2008 Sichuan earthquake.

In addition to his philanthropy, Ma is also known for his charismatic leadership style and his ability to think outside the box. He is known for his unconventional management strategies, such as allowing employees to take a sabbatical every five years, and for his emphasis on innovation and creativity. He has also been recognized for his contributions to the development of the internet and e-commerce in China and around the world.

Ma stepped down as executive chairman of Alibaba in 2019, he remained on the board of directors and continued to be a significant shareholder. Since then, he has continued to be involved in various philanthropic and business endeavors, including the launch of the eWTP (electronic World Trade Platform) and the Jack Ma Rural Teachers Award.

Ma's journey from an English teacher to a business tycoon is a testament to the power of perseverance and determination. His success with Alibaba Group has helped to shape the global economy and has been a major driver of China's economic growth. His philanthropy and leadership have also had a lasting impact on the communities in which he operates. Despite his success, he continues to be a humble and down-to-earth person, always willing to share his knowledge and experience with others. Jack Ma is a true inspiration to many people around the world, especially in poor countries, showing that with hard work and determination, anyone can overcome poverty and achieve success.

WANGARI MAATHAI

"Human rights are not things that are put on the table for people to enjoy. These are things you fight for and then you protect."

— Wangari Maathai

Wangari Maathai in 2005

Wangari Maathai (1940-2011) was a Kenyan environmental and political activist, who was the first African woman to receive the Nobel Peace Prize in 2004. She was a founder of the Green Belt Movement, an environmental organization that has planted over 50 million trees in Kenya since 1977.

Poverty was a significant issue in Wangari Maathai's life, both during her childhood and throughout her career as an environmental and political activist.

Maathai grew up in a rural village Ihithe in Kenya during a time of colonial rule and widespread poverty. Her family was poor and she had to work hard to support herself and her education. Despite these challenges, she was able to receive a good education and eventually earned a PhD in veterinary anatomy from the University of Nairobi.

As an adult, Maathai continued to be deeply affected by the poverty she saw in her country and dedicated her life to addressing it. She saw a connection between poverty and environmental degradation, and believed that environmental conservation could be a powerful tool for combating poverty. Through her work with the Green Belt Movement, she sought to promote sustainable land use and provide resources for local communities, such as food, fuel, and income.

In 1977, Maathai founded the Green Belt Movement, which aimed to address the issues of poverty, deforestation, and environmental degradation in Kenya. The organization focused on planting trees and promoting sustainable land use, as well as empowering women to take control of their own lives and resources. She believed that by providing women with training and resources, they could take on leadership roles in their communities and improve their own lives and the lives of their families. Through her work with the Green Belt Movement, she empowered thousands of women to become leaders in their communities.

Maathai's work had a significant impact in reducing poverty and improving the lives of the people in Kenya. The trees planted by the organization helped to combat deforestation and soil erosion, and also provided food, fuel, and income for local communities.

Her efforts also extended to politics and human rights. She was an advocate for democracy and human rights in

Kenya, and was a member of the Kenyan parliament from 2002 to 2007. Maathai also served as an assistant minister in the Kenyan government, and was appointed as a Deputy Minister for Environment, Natural Resources and Wildlife in 2003.

Eventually, she was recognized internationally, and in 2004 she became the first African woman to receive the Nobel Peace Prize for her "contribution to sustainable development, democracy and peace". She used the prize money to establish the Wangari Maathai Foundation, which continues to promote her vision of environmental conservation and sustainable development.

In addition to the Nobel Peace Prize, Maathai also received many other awards and honors throughout her life, including the Right Livelihood Award, the Order of the Golden Ark, and the Tyler Prize for Environmental Achievement.

Maathai passed away in 2011, but her legacy lives on through the Green Belt Movement and the many other organizations that have been inspired by her work. Her vision of using environmental conservation to combat poverty, promote sustainable development, and empower women continues to be an important one in many parts of the world.

Conclusion

Obstacles to success come in many forms, and each individual may face different challenges depending on their circumstances. Some of the most common ones were noted and the individuals who in real life overcame the challenges are learnt and hope their life stories inspire you long to achieve greatness in everyone's life. I recommend reading more on the individuals' life stories as suitable to you.

Disability: Individuals with disabilities may face additional challenges in achieving success due to physical or cognitive limitations. They may have difficulty accessing education and job opportunities, as well as navigating societal attitudes and discrimination. However, with the proper support and accommodations, people with disabilities can overcome these obstacles and achieve success. This can include assistive technology, workplace accommodations, and education accommodations. Additionally, laws such as the Americans with Disabilities Act (ADA) protect the rights of individuals with disabilities in the workplace and in education.

Age: For older individuals who may face discrimination in the workforce, it is difficult to pursue greater dreams. Age discrimination can limit job opportunities and advancement, and can make it difficult for older workers to continue to support themselves and their families. However, older individuals can take steps to combat age discrimination, such as by staying current with technology and skills, and by being open to new opportunities.

Negativity: A negative attitude or mindset can also be an obstacle to success. Negative thoughts and beliefs can limit an individual's potential and make it difficult for them to achieve their goals. To overcome this obstacle, individuals can practice positive thinking and visualization, surround themselves with supportive and encouraging people, and seek the help of a therapist or counselor if necessary.

Discrimination: On the basis of race, gender, sexual orientation, religion, or any other characteristic, differentiating people can also be a major obstacle to success. These forms of discrimination can limit access to education, job opportunities, and fair treatment in the workplace. Discrimination can also lead to feelings of self-doubt and low self-esteem. To overcome this, individuals can educate themselves on discrimination and its effects, seek support from friends and allies, and advocate for change in their communities.

Accidents: Whether they are physical or financial, a single accident can change one's entire life. They can result in injuries, medical expenses, and lost income, making it difficult for individuals to maintain their livelihoods. To mitigate the impact of accidents, individuals can take steps to protect themselves, such as by carrying insurance, creating emergency savings, and having a financial plan in place.

Failures: Although it is a natural part of life, it can be a major obstacle to success. Fear of failure can prevent individuals from taking risks and trying new things, which can limit their potential. To overcome this obstacle, individuals can learn to view failure as a learning opportunity and to persevere despite setbacks. They can also practice self-compassion and remind themselves that failure is not a reflection of their worth as a person.

Immigration: It is new world for the immigrants with many challenges such as language barriers, cultural differences, and discrimination. They may also have difficulty finding work, accessing education, and navigating the legal system. To overcome these obstacles, immigrants can learn the language, seek out community support, and educate themselves about their rights and resources.

Poverty: It often limits access to education, resources, and opportunities. However, there are several ways in which individuals can overcome poverty and achieve success: Education, Entrepreneurship, Networking, Access to resources, Mentorship, and Government policies. It's important to note that overcoming poverty is not just an individual effort, systemic and structural changes are necessary to truly address poverty and provide equal opportunities for all.

It's important to remember that success is not always linear, and that setbacks and failures are a natural part of the process. With determination, perseverance, and the right resources and support, anyone can break the rock (won't call it a glass) ceiling like a phoneix, rising from the ashes.

Thanks for reading

www.ingramcontent.com/pod-product-compliance
Lightning Source LLC
Chambersburg PA
CBHW022030150726
47990CB00002B/889